NOTHING
BUT
FAITH

Activating Your Spiritual Stethoscope

D1304464

Connie Ajah-Ayang and Gifty D. Boateng

DEDICATION

To the healthcare professionals who persevered and showed up daily
to help those in need during the pandemic.

ACKNOWLEDGEMENTS

Connie's Acknowledgments:

Never would I have thought that writing a book would be this hard or as rewarding a process. First off, none of this book would have been possible without the Almighty God. Thank you, Lord, for your Faithfulness in my life, for your grace and mercy, and for your precious gift of Salvation that I have come to enjoy in my journey of Faith. Thank you, Lord, for giving me a voice through this inspiring work to share my Faith. Through the Holy Spirit, you inspired us to write this book, and to share our Faith as we navigated the calling of "nurse life" during a Pandemic. Without you Lord, I am nothing!

To my amazing husband, Bruno, thank you for not only believing in me but for also throwing all your weight behind me. In everything I do, you are my number one support. Even though some of my ideas may appear crazy, you are always there to cheer me on! Through the years, you have proven to me that I can always count on you. Thank you for all your love and support.

To my darling sons, Jayden (my baby Jay) and Avery-Jayce (A.J.), you are my precious gifts from God, and I love you both so, so much. You both inspire me every day to be better and to do better in everything I do! I pray that you both will become everything that God has purposed for your lives.

To all my siblings, Kenneth, Derek, Thomas, Mabel, Miriam, and Mercy, I love you all. Thank you for the bond that we share. Thank you for your encouragement, support and love!

To my father, Mr. Ajah E. Bernard of blessed memory, I miss you so much dad. I know you are smiling down on all of us and are proud of what we have become. Please, continue to watch over us. To my beloved mother, Mrs. Ajah E. Lydia, thank you for the Christian values you instilled in my siblings and I. Mamah, you are my hero, my prayer warrior and my friend. I have yet to meet someone with such a strong, unstaggering Faith as yours! Thank you for teaching us that we can't be anything without our Faith in God. Thank you for your endless prayers, and for your unconditional and tough love for my siblings and I, and all your grandchildren! You greatly inspire me in my Faith-filled journey. What would we do without you, Mom? We may not say it often, but you are the best mom!

To my very special and loving uncle, Mr. Godfred E. Mesumbe, how can I say Thank You? You are a man with a heart bigger than life itself. Because of your great desire to be a blessing to others and to see others succeed, you made it possible for us, your nieces and nephews, to migrate to the United States from Cameroon, West Africa. You went to the U.S. before everyone else in the family because you were determined to ensure that all of your "mother's grandchildren" would also get the opportunity to live the "American" dream. You are the reason I am here today!

To my cousins, Ernest and Divine Ebwelle, you are more like brothers to me. I just want to thank you for not only opening your doors to me, when I came to the United States, but for also helping me navigate the challenges of adjusting to life here. As well as always supporting me as I found my bearings to establish myself. I really appreciate you both!

To my fellow nurses out there, who showed up every day for your patients, you answered the "call" to fight this war against an unknown enemy and came out as warriors. Despite the many challenges we personally faced during the Pandemic and collectively as a healthcare community, you still fought this battle with resilience, grit and compassion.

You all stood your ground. You all are Superheroes. It is true – "Not all heroes wear capes." Thank you for all your sacrifices!

Finally, I want to say thank you to our publishing team at Victorious You Press! Thank you for taking a chance on us. Thank you for helping us author and publish our first book. We are greatly indebted to you all!

Gifty's Acknowledgments:

First, I want to the thank the Holy Spirit, who is my constant companion and advocate. I can't do anything without the Power Of God. I thank God for my gifts, his grace, my life and my calling to work in his vineyard. He is the source of my strength, hope, joy, faith and peace. Everything that I Am and Will Become is because I know whom he has called/chosen me to be. Nothing, but God!

To my four brothers, Kingsley, Francis, Isaac and Charles, thank you for your support, encouragement, motivation and love. I'm truly blessed to have such amazing brothers in my world.

To my parents, Mr. and Mrs. Fordjour, thank you for instilling in my siblings and I's early years to always PUT GOD FIRST, the Power of prayer and your unconditional love. I remember most mornings before going to school mom would drag us to church for prayers. "Train up a child in the way he should go, and when he is old, he will not depart from it." (Proverbs 22:6, NKJV). Thank you both for naming me GIFTY, which means a gift from God. My name constantly reminds me Who I am and Whose I am. I pray that I will always remain in Him, so that he can also always remain in me. So, Help Me, God!

To my wonderful husband, thank you for your prayers, support, advice and love. Thank you for always challenging me to do more.

To my precious gifts from God, Samuel and Emmanuella, I love you both so much.

To my nieces and nephews, I hope you continue to allow God to instruct your steps.

To my In-Laws, thank you for your love and support.

To my Sisters United In Prayer (S.U.I.P.), thank you for always uniting us in prayer. Indeed, prayer is the master's key to unlocking the door.

To my church, The Apostolic Church International, thank you for always teaching me to be steadfast in prayer and the Word of God. You continue to sharpen my prayers and spiritual life. I am moving in the Holy Sprit's Power and In the Right Direction. So, Help Me, God.

To my co-workers, PACUTIES, and nurses all over the world, thank you for letting the light of God shine through you every day especially during our darkest days of Covid. You allowed God to use you and to be with you. You never gave up. Thank you!

To 3G Purely Inspirational Network, thank you for always teaching me to "Let the redeemed of the Lord say so." (Psalm 107:2, NKJV). I'm saying so. In Jesus name, Amen!

And to you, the reader, thank you for inviting us into your life. We pray and trust that you will activate your spiritual stethoscope in your workplace, home, and life.

THE SIGNIFICANCE OF THE STETHOSCOPE

What is a Stethoscope, and Why is it Important?

You would hardly find a nurse, a doctor, or a respiratory therapist without a Stethoscope hung around their necks while at work. But what exactly is a Stethoscope?

The stethoscope is a device that helps physicians or other healthcare providers such as nurses listen to the internal organs, such as lungs, heart, and bowel sounds, and it is also used to check blood pressure. In addition, it helps to amplify internal sounds. With the help of the stethoscope, which has become the symbol of the medical profession, the providers can quickly ascertain what is wrong with a patient and initiate the appropriate plan of care for that patient.

The use of the stethoscope is to help the nurse discern...

1. What's inside? What's going on with the patient?

2. The status of the internal organs, and

3. Based on the findings, it informs the medical professional of the proper direction/treatment for the patient.

Spiritually, as nurses and or healthcare workers, we need to know precisely what is happening around us, be it at work or home. It is essential that we connect with God spiritually for the right discernment of our everyday life and not just when we are in a crisis mode. God speaks to us all the time, but we are not listening, and part of the reason is that we have not developed or activated our spiritual stethoscope. When our minds and hearts are clear, we will hear God's voice speaking; He's an OMNIPRESENCE AND OMNISCIENCE GOD!!

As we wrestle with this pandemic, it becomes more and more evident that we have no choice but to activate our Spiritual Stethoscope. We must initiate prayer, praise, worship, and meditate on the word of God daily. This posture is not only for direction but to surrender our day into God's hands, with Him leading and guiding us along the way.

TABLE OF CONTENTS:

INTRODUCTION:

"WHAT HAPPENS WHEN THE ONE CALLED TO GIVE HOPE NEEDS HOPE?"

A s nurses, we are being called to be agents of hope, healing and encouragement. We are of the few professions – if not the only profession – that are called to carry out the very core of Jesus's teachings: to love our neighbors, to care for and comfort the sick, and to give hope to the Hopeless in times of despair. "In fact, Florence Nightingale, who is often revered as the pioneer of modern-day nursing, exemplifies what it means to practice Jesus's teachings. She first gained prominence when she led a group of nurses to staff an overseas hospital during the Crimean war of 1854. When she and her team arrived, they noticed the conditions of the hospital were deplorable. It was overcrowded. Patients were covered in dirty rags; the water was contaminated and the overall sanitary conditions were disgusting. She and her team got to work. They cleaned and sanitized the hospital wards, bathed patients and did their laundry. She knew that these patients would heal better and quicker if their environment was more comfortable." (Winkelstein 2009, 311) Florence Nightingale did what, nurses, do daily. We are the ones, who are blessed and privileged enough, to help with ushering God's magnificent creations. We are privileged to be there from the time of their births, their very first cries into the world, and we are there to close their eyes when they take their last breaths.

Most times, this job can be emotionally draining, but it is a blessing to be able to carry out such a service to others. Nurses are called to be caring and nurturing, but what happens when the one called to give hope needs hope? What happens when nurses are expected to be hopeful? What happens when nurses, who give hope and encouragement to others, need that same hope and encouragement reciprocated back to them to keep their mind, physical body and spirit together – not just for themselves or their families or their communities, but also for their nation!

This happened to nurses in 2020. It became clear that 2020 was not only the year of the nurse, but also the year of a Global Pandemic. The world needed nurses more than ever. As nurses, we were called to be at the battle's forefront. We were called to fight in a battlefield where we weren't supplied with the right weapons to fight or protect ourselves with. We also didn't have that much information about this deadly virus that had ignited and is still causing a global pandemic. We were all just learning as we went. We were trying every treatment possible. We were hoping that it would help stop the virus. All our treatments were like throwing spaghetti on a wall and hoping that it would stick. We had no treatment plan or vaccine to prevent this virus. The medical community was and is still baffled by this unknown enemy.

My co-author Gifty and I, as children of God, knew we had no choice but to turn to our source of hope and healing – our Faith in God. That is the reason we are writing this book and dedicating it to all the healthcare workers, especially nurses, who have been on the front lines fighting this pandemic. We want you to have a set of tips and tools for a firm foundation in Faith (also known as the triple F's) for when you venture into the Lion's den. Despite this mountain or even another healthcare crisis, your Faith will be so steadfast that you will continue to confess the Word of God and His promises.

We hope this book will offer you a blueprint of how you can overcome your challenges through Faith. We also want to assure you, our readers, that the despair and helplessness felt by many and also the great losses that we have encountered cannot undermine our hope. In times of hardships, trials or challenges, remember that there is a higher power who is a source of comfort and strength that we can look up to – that higher power is **God!** We want you to know that you can hold on to your Faith even during these trying times. We want to encourage you to step into your Faith and excel in your career. We also want to remind you that God has so many promises (be it professionally or personally) for you. And as you navigate this life, remember that you can always lean on those promises to encourage you to keep your head high, your chin up and be the champions and warriors that you were born to be for answering the call of this Noble Profession of Nursing.

CHAPTER 1:

STORIES OF PERSEVERANCE AND SUR-VIVAL THROUGH THE PANDEMIC

Section One:
Connie Ajah-Ayang's Story

For starters, I am not an ordained pastor. I am not a minister in a church. I am only someone who performs regular work, while every day being a child of God. His grace is more than sufficient for me. I was empowered by His Grace with inspiration from the Holy Spirit to share my story, and work on this inspirational piece with my friend and co-author, Gifty.

My name is Connie Ajah-Ayang. I am a wife, a mother of two adorable sons, and a sister to six siblings. I am also blessed to be an aunt to my three lovely nieces and nephews. I have also been a nurse for the past 13 years now, and I am currently working as a clinical Informatics Nurse. I'm not very involved with direct patient care, so my story differs from someone who works directly with patients – like my friend and co-author, Gifty. However, with the Pandemic, we were all affected and impacted by the uncertain circumstances in caring for patients.

If you ask any nurse or healthcare worker what it was like working in the year 2020, I bet we'd all say it was quite a year, and quite the journey. It was full of so much uncertainty, and many of us have our own stories to tell.

I remember clearly how excited I was on New Years' Eve. Oh, I was excited about how we were about to step into 2020! It was going to be a big celebration, and the excitement seen around the world was palpable. It's hard for me to remember ever being that excited about a new year before. One of my new year goals was to intentionally do everything I planned to do! I said to myself, 'It's the beginning of a new decade, and so everything I do will have a meaningful impact on my life and my family's lives for the rest of this new decade.' It was the year that I had planned to set the pace for my life and for the rest of this decade. Like many of us, I had hopes, goals and exciting plans for my family, myself and my career.

But the one who holds the universe in His palms had other plans for me, my fellow nurses and the world at large. As we began the year, the coronavirus emerged, and like every other healthcare organization, we braced ourselves for the unknown. By the middle of January, we started hearing news of a certain type of emergent strand of the Corona Virus coming from China called Corona Virus or COVID-19. At the time, we knew that it was very contagious, and easily got people sick with a potential for death. By the end of January, the government had reported the first cases of Covid in the United States. In March, our state, Delaware, reported its first presumptive positive case. At the hospital, we started screening and paying close attention to patients who had traveled out of the country from China within the last two weeks. We specifically screened these patients for the Covid-19 symptoms. Things were rapidly changing. My fellow nurses and I were even more cautious. With cautious optimism, we believed it would not be as bad as it first seemed. But then, our patient screenings were later extended to anyone who had traveled out of the United States.

It's not the first time a pandemic has hit the world. In 1918, there was the Spanish Flu that lasted from 1918-1920, but the reality is that most of us living today have experienced nothing like this. Soon, it was bad news after bad news, and watching the news became depressing.

Everything had come to a halt, but not the lives or jobs of essential workers. By March 2020, the World Health Organization had declared that we were battling a global pandemic. Our nation was on lockdown. In fact, Covid shut the entire world down. With everything coming to a halt, my fellow nurses and I had to rise to our Calling while also being Enough for ourselves, our families and our communities. Some of us had to become teachers or coaches for our school-age children, while also working eight or twelve hours shifts. My fellow nurses and I definitely seemed to have gained some sort of superpower during this pandemic. And that's not even all of it. Our Calling had become a matter of literally putting our lives and those of our family members at risk. And sadly, we lost so many fellow nurses, healthcare workers and their families to this deadly pandemic.

You know, I was in my late 30s when I really came to know God. You can know religion and church. You can even be familiar with God. But until you know God like you know your parents or your best friend, it isn't enough. It's not the same. That's how it was for me.Growing up, I knew of God, but I didn't know God. I was raised to understand religion. I went to an all-girls Catholic boarding school, and at some point, I even considered being a nun, but I was lacking in my relationship with God. I didn't know God on a personal level until 2017. That was when I encountered God, and knew God on a personal level. That year was also when I understood that I could have G.O.D. (God On Demand) whenever and wherever I needed to. I began to develop a closely-knit relationship with God to the extent that, wherever or whenever I needed Him, I could just sit in time and connect with him. The same Spirit that was promised to the apostles was in me from the day I accepted Jesus Christ as the Lord and Savior of my life. And you know, we can never "know enough of God" because as we develop our relationship with Him, there is so much more to still learn about how awesome our God really is. He is excellent and mighty. Anyway, I digress.

As the pandemic raged on, I had to have a conversation with God. I had to call him "On Demand." I had to speak with Him and hear from Him. Thinking back to that day, I remember saying, "God, here's the deal, I'm scared. I'm trying not to be, but I am. I know I shouldn't be because as a child of God, why should I fear, right? I feel like I should be bigger or stronger by now, but I'm not. Lord, I'm afraid that I'll do everything that I possibly can to protect me and my family, but that it still won't be enough. I'm afraid of someone I love getting sick or possibly dying from the Coronavirus. I'm afraid that the world will not be the same as we know it to be." I was also afraid that my life was always going to feel a little uneasy because of the uncertainty surrounding our current crisis. I'm scared, in fact, I am terrified. And can I tell you that we become our thoughts.

Not long after this conversation with God, my fears became my reality. My fears had manifested in ways beyond my control and took hold of me. My fear had overcome me. I was like Job, who also had his fears manifested. In Job 3:25 (NIV), he cries out, "What I feared has come upon me; what I dreaded has happened to me." Looking back, my situation was a reminder that amid the chaos or challenges, we ought to be careful of the thoughts we entertain since we become what we think. The bible says, "as a man thinketh in his heart, so is he." (Proverbs 23:7, KJV) I learned this the hard way, and unfortunately, so very often too. It's a fact that if we don't take control of our thoughts then we can't take control of our lives. Therefore, it's very important for us to understand that the truest things about us are what God says they are. Anything else or anything less is False. Until we take control of our thoughts and words, we can't take back control of our lives, and truly live in the Purpose for which we were created!

I remember one evening watching the news, and it was reported that a lady whose husband and son both died from Covid were laid to rest at a funeral home. I watched as she couldn't control her tears. She was in pain. And what pained me the most was the fact that she couldn't even have a regular funeral because of the covid restrictions in place. She was all by herself with only a handful of people to comfort her. The Coronavirus took away any semblance of normalcy even in mourning the loss of loved ones. COVID-19 didn't just take away liberties that we took for granted like hugging friends or family. It also took away the comfort and support we receive from friends and family in times of grief. That news scene was like the situations of the patients we admitted for the Coronavirus. No one could have visitors, so often patients died with no family present. It was painful. That scenario put a range in my heart. I was in it as I watched them die alone, and it left me heartbroken.

Not long after, I got sick. I was at work one afternoon when I suddenly started feeling feverish. I brushed it off as just chills. Then, I started to feel warm on my body. I decided to go to the nurses' station to get a thermometer and take my temperature. It was a low-grade fever. All of a sudden, I felt this metallic taste in my mouth. Then, I remembered my coffee that morning tasted weird. But I thought, "maybe my husband, who buys my coffee every morning, mistakenly bought the wrong flavor. I called him to inquire, but he assured me he got my usual. Later that day, I decided to get food from the cafeteria just so I could test out what was up with my taste buds. When I ate the food, I just knew something was definitely not right. I had lost my sense of taste. I panicked. I called my manager and explained how I was feeling. She asked me to call the Occupational health office and then go home.

My fears became a reality. I had the Coronavirus. I was terrified. I stayed home for two weeks. This period was particularly hard on my kids, as they could not come near me. Thank God for my husband, who had to take off work to be with me and take care of the kids. Since this was before a vaccine, I could only continue whatever home remedy treatment my mom and I could come up with. I also stayed prayed-up.

As I was meditating on scripture one day, I recalled that, just before I got sick, about a week earlier, an older lady friend of mine from church who had never called me before had called me out of the blue. She called to check up on me and my family. She asked how everyone was doing with everything that was going on. I told her I was at work. She then asked what I did because almost everyone was at home, except the essential workers. I told her I was a nurse. Then, she offered to pray for me. She prayed that God protect me and my family from this infection. She then prayed that "...even if I got sick, it will not be unto death..." citing the scripture in the story of Lazarus – in which Jesus raises a man from the dead. (John 11:4, KJV). I know her call was divinely orchestrated to save me from this illness. Even now, I still believe her prayers saved my life. And then it clicked, "God got me." I was not alone in this. I knew that if He brought me to it, He will bring me through it.

As children of God, we are not excluded from all the challenges that happen to people, but what is different and makes us distinct is that through the challenges of life God is with us. We are never alone. With

God on our side, we shall overcome. Soon after I resumed work, my oldest son got sick. He displayed all the symptoms, including pneumonia. Watching my child suffer from this illness had me feeling helpless. It's the worst feeling ever, and I feared the worst. I prayed, "Oh, God, save my child!" Thank God he answered my prayers.

It was then that I realized that I couldn't go into this war zone armed with only the physical weapons of PPE (personal protective equipment). This, to me, was not only a physical war. It was also a spiritual battle, and obviously I needed to have the right weapons to fight with. And just like that, I had no other choice but to activate my Spiritual Stethoscope.

I needed something to lean on. We all do sometimes, especially when facing such uncertainty. I needed something that would give me hope. I needed something that would strengthen me. I needed something that would give me the courage to fight faithfully without fear of my opponent. I had to have something that reminded me of who and whose I was. That something, to me, was my Faith in God! I had to turn to the true source of my hope, protection and healing. I had to believe that God "...has not given us a spirit of fear, but of power and of love and of a sound mind." (2 Timothy 1:7, NKJV).

As the coronavirus spread faster than we thought, my state and fellow healthcare organizations put in place strategies to control the virus. One strategy involved statewide screening and testing, which our organization did in the community in partnership with the state. I was part of the team that was deployed to provide community screening, education and testing through the drive-through clinic in our city. As we all know, our Faith is not something commonly talked about in the workplace. We consider it a very personal topic. However, I remember that something – I believe it was the Holy Spirit – pushed me to not be afraid to bring up prayer and praying with others as we were served our community.

Everything about the coronavirus was unknown. Scientists and researchers were busy working around the clock to get a treatment, and possibly even a cure for this unknown enemy. And maybe we once believed that healthcare professionals could cure people who were sick, but Coronavirus opened our eyes. The ability to heal and the power of healing does not come from us, but from God. We had to look to God to not only heal our patients, but also for protection from this infection and for guidance in providing the right care.

Whenever I was working at the clinic site, I invited my co-workers to join me in prayer before we started our day. I prayed for God's protection over us and the community. I also prayed for peace amid so much uncertainty. Soon, I caught notice that it wasn't just us, but also so many other healthcare workers praying in hospitals or outside of hospitals all over the nation. They were calling on the healing power of God from this pandemic.

Yes, we had our PPE (personal protective equipment) on, and took all the precautions that science told us to practice to prevent contracting the virus, but I still believe that I couldn't rely on just PPE and precautions to save me from not getting sick. I knew, and I know that the Power in the precious blood of Jesus Christ keeps protecting me from this illness. So yes, we should exercise caution, but we also need to apply God's wisdom to the situation. We need to hold onto our Faith to make it through this crisis. Our Faith does not become alive until we act on God's promises to us, and we find those promises in His word!

As challenging as our job is, we, too, need a daily dose of inspiration. Something uplifting that will help us pull through the difficult and hard times. We hope this book will not only remind you of God's promises to you, but also inspire you to keep ongoing. Hold onto your faith in challenging and uncertain times, and remember to stand on a firm foundation of faith, as we continue today to navigate these uncertain times.

Section Two:
Gifty D. Boateng's Story

Throughout our lives, we face challenges in many types of situations and during different seasons in our lives. Every day is a new day with our God. His mercies are fresh every morning. In Psalm 34:19 (NKJV) scripture states, "Many are the afflictions of the righteous, but the Lord delivers him out of all."

I want to introduce myself as a Nurse in the vineyard of the Lord. My name is Gifty Boateng. I am a daughter of the Most High. I am a wife, a mother of two miracle babies, Samuel and Emmanuella, a sister to four wonderful brothers, an auntie and a friend to many. My nursing career in this noble profession spans as far back as seventeen years ago. I have worked in a Medical-Surgical Unit, a Long-term facility and now I currently work as a clinical coordinator in the Post Anesthesia Care Unit.

During the end of 2019, I faced a major health crisis which required a surgical procedure. During my recovery period, I got to spend more time in the word of God. I reflected on his purpose and unmerited favor in my life. My mindset started shifting to focus more on the work of God and his purpose for my life in this world.

I then went back to work over nine weeks post-surgery. In December 2019, I started sharing how the World Health Organization had declared 2020 as the "Year of the Nurse and Midwife." I was excited of the light being shone on nurses and the nursing profession, which has been the heart and center of the healthcare community for a while now, but little did we know what we were about to face.

I co-founded an organization called the Noble Nurses Network. Our vision is to bring nurses together through empowerment, encouragement, education and giving back to the community. There is and continues to be an issue with nurses committing suicide. On top of nurses also experiencing an increase in job burnout Our first event, the Nightingale Nurses Ball, was supposed to be a night of empowerment and self-care for nurses in the state of Delaware. We had sponsors and the venue was secured. The event was set to go in March 2020, but then we went into a national lockdown.

My co-workers and I were so terrified and anxious about what we were hearing in the media, and seeing in our workplaces about this monster disease called Covid-19. There was so much that was unknown. There were a lot of tears and mental breakdowns. We had to quickly adapt to the frequent updates in protocols, practices and stressful shift changes in our workplaces. Many healthcare organizations were facing PPE and bed shortages. And school children were placed in remote learning.

My husband and I are essential workers, so we knew that this was going to be tough on us. I was also worried about both my parents and four siblings because they lived in the Epicenter of the pandemic (New York City), and being unable to assist or visit them made things much worse for me. This was very hard! Elective surgeries at work were being cancelled, and many of my co-workers were being deployed to other departments or to the community Covid testing sites.

During these uncertain times, I realized then that 'Nothing, but God & Faith' could protect and save us from the arms of Covid-19. I remembered what David said in Psalms 23:4 (NKJV), "Yea, though I walk through the valley of the shadow of death, I will fear no evil; for You are with me; Your rod and Your staff, they comfort me." It became more meaningful to me to know that when I'm facing a challenging time that I should rely on my firm foundation in faith and in the word of God.

The prophet Isaiah proclaims in Isaiah 41:13 (NKJV), "For I, the Lord your God, will hold your right hand, saying to you, 'Fear not, I will help you.'" It's a reminder to us all that God will help us. I also want you to know that, as the late Evangelist Billy Graham proclaimed, "The WILL OF GOD will never take you where the GRACE OF GOD will not PROTECT YOU." Therefore, it's important that we allow the Holy Spirit to fill and use us as God's chosen servants.

In Proverb 3:5-6 (NKJV), scripture states, "Trust in the Lord with all your heart, And lean not on your own understanding; In all your ways acknowledge Him, And He shall direct your paths." This scripture means that we should recognize that God is God and acknowledge His authority over all things. We should keep Him as the center point of all that we do. The word of God instructs us to meditate on his word – day and night. His word is a lamp that lights our path. As nurses and healthcare workers called and chosen by the Most High God to serve our patients and communities, we must activate our spiritual stethoscopes daily and especially during difficult situations like these.

During this storm of Covid, I lifted my eyes to heaven – where our help comes from. Our Help/Hope only comes from the maker of heaven and earth. At my workplace, we also turned our eyes to the maker. We turned to our Faith and activated our spiritual weapons through prayer and worship. Many healthcare providers posted on different social media platforms their pictures of them praying and singing on rooftops, nursing units or in their communities.

Looking back, I remember a physician whom I worked with had messaged me on Facebook about praying at work before starting our day. To tell you the truth, I was a little hesitant about doing that at work and with other people present, but then I realized that God had placed me in this moment and season for his glory to prevail. Like I said earlier, most of my co-workers were very terrified and scared of the unknown, but we knew that Prayer was the key to opening the doors for us to see our way through.

As a nurse of faith, I went to work every day without calling out even once because I knew that I had put on my Full Armor of GOD. With His armor, I knew that I could "stand against the wiles of the devil." (Ephesians 6:11, NKJV). Scripture tells us that when David was about to face the giant Goliath, he knew that Goliath would go against him with a sword, a spear and a javelin, but David went against this giant in the name of the Lord Almighty. Every shift felt like my co-workers and I were about to face Goliath, but we placed our Trust and Hope in God's hands. Relying solely on our PPE for protection was not enough. We relied on the Almighty God for his PPE over our families, coworkers and ourselves.

In April 2020, the favor of the Lord was upon me. I found myself on the front page of a local newspaper about the Noble Nurses Network. I was also on the front page of my state's newspaper as well as our organization's media page for that week. This was nothing, but God's blessings. Even in the middle of the storm, He remains God.

A famous lyrist, Edward Mote, once wrote, "My Hope is built on nothing less than Jesus's blood and righteousness (On Christ the Solid Rock We Stand)." When we face trials and tribulations in life, let us build on Christ the Solid Rock when all other ground is sand. We'll continue to hold onto our Faith while we activate our spiritual stethoscopes. This book is the survival kit to help you hold onto your faith and purpose as you're called & chosen to serve others.

Chapter Reflection:

What was the year 2020 like for you? And what was the most im-portant lesson(s) you learned?

CHAPTER 2:

WHAT IS FAITH?

Co-author, Gifty Boateng, believes that, "Faith is the basic ingredient to begin a relationship with God." Co-author, Connie Ajah-Ayang, believes that, "Faith is believing that God has done what He says He has done, and Trusting that He will do what He says He will do." Through their faith, the people in the bible earned a good reputation with God, and in turn earned God's love because of their belief. Connie Ajah-Ayang cites Hebrews 11:1-3 (NLT), "Faith shows the reality of what we hope for; and it is the evidence of things we cannot see." With faith, we understand that the entire universe was formed at God's command, and that what we now see did not come from anything that could be seen when God made it.

Co-author Connie Ajah-Ayang continues, "We often hear the word 'Faith' used in so many catch phrases or hashtags like, 'Have Faith. It will work out. Keep the Faith. Walk by Faith, and Not by Sight. Faith over Fear. Faith it 'til you make it, etc.' But what does the word, Faith, really mean? What does it mean to have Faith? "The word, Faith, derives from the Latin word, fides, which means the confidence or trust in a person, thing, or concept." (2019, par.1) In a religious context, Faith means a belief in a higher power (be it God, Spirits or people), or in the doctrines and/or teachings of a religion or faith-based community.

Essentially, Faith means a belief: to have confidence with a firm conviction in someone or something. For example, you might often hear people say, "I have faith in my spouse or in my best friend." Those people are expressing that they carry a confidence and trust in that specific person that is not so easily broken. It is an unshakable trust. Those people are also expressing that no matter what happens they fully commit to the belief that they can truly rely on that person to be loyal and faithful. Those people trust their loved ones to come through for them and to always have their backs irrespective of the circumstances. Their loved ones will always be there for them and vice versa. This is what Faith is all about!

Faith is the confidence and trust in someone. In a religious context, Faith is the belief that God is working things out on our behalf even when we cannot see it for ourselves. Yes, even when we cannot see God, it doesn't mean that He is absent. Yes, even when it feels like we cannot feel Him, it doesn't mean that He isn't there. God is always present, even in the most difficult moments or situations we may find ourselves in. The Bible is always a good reminder of God's constant presence and goodness in our lives. In Psalm 23:6 (NKJV), the scripture states, "Surely goodness and mercy shall follow me All the days of my life; And I will dwell in the house of the Lord Forever." And in that same scripture, Psalm 23:4 (NKJV), David states, "Yea, though I walk through the valley of the shadow of death, I will fear no evil; For You are with me..." Why does David say that? Because he had Faith in God and knew that God was always with him – like He is with us!

Co-author Connie Ajah-Ayang professes, "I am the type of woman who draws my strength from my Faith in God. What that means, to me, is believing that God has done what He says He has done, and also trusting that He will do exactly what He says He will do! Scripture told us that God created the World with only His Words. Without a doubt, I believe that because I see His creation all around me. My very existence is proof of His Work. I am His creation. And so, if He proclaims that He has specific plans for my life and my future, whether or not I know of those plans, I will believe in Him! I will hold on to the truth that I am *"faithing it until I make it"* because those are His words! That is what Faith means to me. Faith is the assurance that the truths revealed and promised in the word of God are true even though most of God's work happens unseen. I have a conviction that my expectations in faith will come to pass – no matter the circumstances I am going through or the circumstances I may encounter in the future."

In Hebrews 11:1 (NKJV), Faith is, "...the substance of things hoped for, the evidence of things not seen." Faith is believing before seeing! Co-author Connie Ajah-Ayang continues, "I'm very fond of saying, 'Faith is my bridge to tomorrow.' Faith guides me into a tomorrow that I might be uncertain of. No one knows what tomorrow may bring or even what's going to happen in the next hour, but because I have faith, I believe that I will not only get to see tomorrow but that it will also be better than today." Believing in someone or something is a good start to having Faith. And when you *know* Faith that is where trust begins. As Dr. Martin Luther King Jr. declared, "Faith is taking the first step even when you don't see the whole staircase." Essentially, Faith is hoping and believing in something even if we don't see it! Faith is acting on God's Words, and letting His Words guide us even when we don't know where He will take us. There is no room for doubt or negativity in Faith.

If we really want to enjoy the eminent grace of the full assurance of faith, then we need to do what Scripture tells us. First, we must believe in the Word of God. Next, we must receive the Word of God in our spirit/soul. Lastly, we must act on the Word of God. In Romans 10:17

(NKJV), "Faith comes by hearing the Word of God." You can't only be-lieve. You have to also receive the Word of God, and act. And remember, Faith is only a word, if we don't follow through and act on it. In James 2:17 (NKJV), scripture states, "...faith by itself, if it does not have works, is dead." Our Faith isn't activated until we believe and trust in the Word of God, and commit ourselves to carrying out His Works. As you read God's promises in His Word, say those scriptures aloud to yourself so that you can hear yourself say them. Then, receive His Word and act on it. You will ensure that the promises He speaks about manifest them-selves in your life. All three elements – listen, receive, act – must go to-gether. And when we take every opportunity to exercise our Faith in God's Word, we see God move on our behalf and in so many ways for us!

Imagine a three-legged stool. Now, imagine a stool with only one leg. It's impossible, right? A stool with only one leg doesn't exist. It can't! The stool would never stand properly without falling. It also wouldn't be able to support someone trying to sit down. The different stools are similar to how different people practice their Faith. For some, practicing their Faith means only listening. For others, practicing their Faith means only acting. But, to truly immerse yourself in your Faith, you need to practice all three in motion. The three legged-stool represents a fulfilling journey in Faith. One leg stands for Belief. Another for Act. And the final one stands for Receive. Alone, each leg, will always be missing something to make it whole, but when you put all three legs of the stool together then you have a Faith that Delivers! Your Faith will stand firm despite the winds of your circumstances or the storms in your life. Your Faith will not shake nor stagger amid adversity. When you operate in that kind of Faith, you don't get caught up in every little detail or distracted by the nuances of life, instead; you get up and Move! When you don't have a clear picture of what lies ahead, you still Move! And when you Move, God will fill in the blank spaces. Just keep going, and don't look back!

In 2 Peter 1:5-6 (NASB), Peter states, "Now for this very reason also, applying all diligence, in your faith supply moral excellence, and in your moral excellence, knowledge, and in your knowledge, self-control, and in your self-control, perseverance, and in your perseverance, godliness." What does it mean to "give all diligence?" It means ensuring or putting in every effort that *your* faith is the right type of faith. The type of faith that is not just a mere belief or doctrine. The type of faith that also depends on God, and on God alone. The type of faith that the gospels of Matthew (17:20, NIV), Mark (4:30-32, NIV) and Luke (17:6, NIV) tell us is as small as a mustard seed but big enough to move mountains, become the largest of all garden plants, and grow tall mulberry trees.

When you walk in that kind of Faith, you will notice a shift in your outlook. Your demeanor will change from one of hopelessness to one of hope. You will know in whom you have to believe in. You will now know that God has you! You will be "faith-knowing!" Co-author Connie Ajah-Ayang defines *"Faith-knowing"* as the level of faith that the patriarch of faith, Abraham, had towards God. When God asked Abraham to sacrifice his son – the son he had prayed so much to have – Abraham answered the call without hesitation. Why did he do that? Because he knew His God. And so will you. Despite whatever situation comes – the doctor's report is troubling, your marriage situation is getting worse or your shift is not going as planned – at the end of the day you will know and believe that God will provide for you and see you to a better tomorrow.

Chapter Reflection:

What does faith mean to you? And how can you hold on to it?

CHAPTER 3:

WHY IS FAITH IMPORTANT?

"To one who has faith, no explanation is necessary.

To one without faith, no explanation is possible."

St. Thomas Aquinas

Faith is not just a Word. It is a belief. Many people exercise some form of Faith in the world. However, some of those people limit their trust in Faith because of what they can achieve on their own, and so, they place little to no Faith in others – including God. Co-author, Connie Ajah-Ayang, says, "I have personally found that placing my Faith in others – especially God – has enabled me to navigate the challenging phases of my life. I can navigate my life a little more effortlessly than if I solely depended on my own ability to fight and overcome my challenges. This type of trust in Faith has allowed me to live my life with more purpose and meaning. I no longer question 'Why?' or 'How?' I just say Yes.' Because trusting and believing in Faith is saying 'Yes' without even knowing why, how or when."

St. Thomas Aquinas proclaimed, "No explanation is necessary, to one who has faith. To one without faith, no explanation is possible." It is impossible to explain what having Faith is to someone. Everyone's experience with their Faith is different. And at the very heart of it, Faith is something rooted deep down in our Souls/Spirits that manifests itself in our everyday actions towards ourselves and others. Faith is a conviction that we not only believe in, but also feel as well.

We all know that life is not always easy. At times, it is full of difficulties. Sometimes, we are on a mountaintop. We are at our peaks, and everything is going well. Sometimes, we are deep down in a valley. We don't know how or where to go next. We are lost. In our lives, we will all go through dark moments or seasons. Sometimes, life just seems like a continuous circle of challenges. You are either going through a challenge, about to go through a challenge, or getting out of a challenge. Either way, we will all face trials at some point in our lives – that is just a given. And it is during those uncertain and bleak times, that we often tend to lose Faith – not just in ourselves, but in others as well. It is in those uncertain moments that we cannot afford to lose our Faith in God or in ourselves. During those times, it is important we remember that we need to hold on to our Faith!

God desires to see every one of us caring for each other like nurses' care for their patients. When we display our caring, compassionate, empathetic hearts and also our love for our neighbors, we demonstrate that we are seeking to be like Jesus. At the core of Jesus's ministries and teachings, he commanded us to help and care for the sick, the lonely and the needy. And Nursing is one of the few professions that exemplifies the "art" of caring that Jesus taught to his followers. We are most definitely blessed and opportune to be amongst the chosen few who get to help women create life, hear a child's first breath, comfort someone after an accident or a loss, and sometimes be the only one present when someone takes their final breath. As nurses, we are called to provide not only physical care, but also emotional and spiritual care to our patients. As nurses, we get to live out our faith. Nursing demonstrates that we can't really practice the "art" of nursing without Faith!

When life gets hard, Faith is the knowledge that things will get better. Faith is a deep belief in the good things that will come after your trials. Faith goes way beyond having hope. Faith is hope, but it is also so much more. Faith is the food for our Spirit/Soul. We nourish our Spirits/Souls with Faith. We would be empty without Faith. This is why Faith can't be easily explained or understood. This is why Faith also can't be looked at through a single lens frame.

Without faith, we wouldn't get into our cars and drive off to work knowing that someone could be drunk driving or driving impaired from a long night at work. Without Faith, we wouldn't get in an airplane or trust the unknown pilot to safely fly and navigate the plane. And it's especially important for nurses to have Faith. If we lived without Faith, we wouldn't even be able to carry out our daily tasks like drawing blood samples, inserting an NG tube, easing a patient's pain or just simply making them comfortable. Without Faith to guide us, we would be completely second guessing every single task we do.

Co-author, Connie Ajah-Ayang, states, "I believe that if you don't stand firm on your faith, then you won't stand at all!" Why? Because how we engage daily in our Faith is just as important as the air we breathe. The air nourishes the body just as Faith nourishes our hearts and our Souls. People have moved mountains and seas with their Faith. You can't say that Faith doesn't provide for us. Even when situations seem dire and without end, our Faith will carry us through to tomorrow, the next day and the day after that.

So, let me ask this, 'What do you really have to lose by having Faith and exercising Faith?' Are you ashamed of having Faith because it will bruise your ego? Are you so used to depending on yourself that depending on others is a terrifying experience? Have you been let down by Faith because you didn't get exactly what you wanted? What would happen if you had Faith and put it into practice? I believe that having Faith would provide you with something better than whatever you originally had. Faith would provide you with a solution, a purpose that aligns with your needs, and God's everlasting love. Faith is important, so much so, that it shouldn't be undermined or understated."

It's also important to remember that Faith profoundly shapes the decisions that millions of people make daily about their medical treatments, and in the routine care they receive. Faith often plays a very important role in not only those decisions, but also, in the decisions of the needs of ourselves and our older family members. Most patients believe that Faith is their narrative, and it's up to us as nurses or healthcare workers to provide culturally competent holistic care and patient-centered care. We need to understand their narrative, so that we can better care for every patient.

Chapter Reflection:

How do you align your nursing professional goals with God's purpose

for you?

CHAPTER 4:

OVERCOMING CHALLENGES!

Nursing is hard!

Most days, nurses work an eight, ten or twelve-hour shift. It is not a walk in the park, and those nurses have only suffered more in the wake of Covid-19. Their normal stressful workdays are now brimming over because of the added challenges of caring for the millions of Covid-19 patients in often underfunded and underpaid hospitals.

Life is full of challenges. It is a roller coaster of highs and lows. Some days, you may feel like you have everything under control or you have everything all figured out. On other days, life throws curve balls at you, and you're left scrambling. You ask, "What just happened? What's going on? Why can't I get through this?" Remember, you are not alone. You may be reading this right now and going through challenges of your own – a loss, financial stress, health issues or family problems – but remember, you can rely on your fellow nurses. You are definitely not alone.

As humans, we often allow our stresses, anxieties and fears to run our lives. We worry over every little thing. We even worry about things we have no control over. And when does worrying over every single thing ever help in resolving our problems? Never. But in these difficult times, it's hard to remember that our Faith will overcome all our stresses, anxieties and fears. In times like these, it's hard to remember that it's okay to feel our feelings. For example, feeling frustrated because things haven't been going as planned or distressed from constantly adapting and adjusting to our new normal. You may even feel as if God has forgotten about you. But, please remember, Jesus's words in John 16:33 (NIV), "...in this world you will have trouble. But take heart! I have overcome the world."

Corrie Ten Boom, sums it up nicely, "Worrying is carrying tomorrow's load with today's strength – carrying two days at once. It is moving into tomorrow ahead of time. Worrying doesn't empty tomorrow of its sorrow, it empties today of its strength." So then, why do we even bother with worrying? We know it "empties us" of our strengths and joys. We also know that our worries can manifest themselves into not only mental health issues, but also emotional and physical issues as well which affect our overall wellbeing too. We all know that there's a clear connection between stress and an increased likelihood of disease and illness in our bodies, but we most often forget that our Faith helps us to keep those issues away. Remember, "If you do not stand firm on your faith, you will not stand at all!" So again, why do we even bother with worrying when we can pray instead?

It's through prayer and Faith that our situations change and improve, even when we have no reason to believe that things will get better or we don't see a way out of our circumstance(s). It is vitally crucial that we, as nurses, learn to harbor Faith in our hearts, and use our Faith to eliminate our stresses, anxieties and fears. One way to do this is to think back on a past situation when you made it through something you thought was impossible. It wasn't. You believed, and good things happened or things got better. You survived. This isn't advice encouraging you to ignore your problems. This is guidance encouraging you to accept your problems, and know that deep down in your heart and Soul/Spirit that your problems will improve. They will not stay bad. Remember to think positive thoughts. Remember to be hopeful. And remember, soon enough, you will see positive outcomes in your life. And if you need help, there are multiple pictures and videos on social media showing healthcare workers all over the world praying, singing and worshipping together. All over the world, healthcare workers also rely on our sustainer, helper, provider, healer, dependable and all-knowing God!

When we hold onto our Faith, no challenge is too difficult. In Mark 9:23, Mark informs us that "If you can believe, all things are possible to him who believes." The key words are "all things." Mark didn't say that some things are possible. No, he said that "all things are possible." Just believe!

It is important to understand that our ability to overcome challenges depends on how we choose to respond to those challenges. We may either embrace our challenges with perseverance as the scripture teaches, in James 1:12 (NIV), "Blessed is the one who perseveres under trial because, having stood the test, that person will receive the crown of life that the Lord has promised to those who love him." In James 1:12 (NIV), we're taught to learn and grow from our experiences. Or we may ignore our challenges, and choose instead to bury our feelings, go about our lives and carry with us a resentment towards God during every moment of the challenge.

Our responses and reactions to our challenges are important. For example, two people can go through the same life challenges – the same unexpected events in life – and come out as completely different people because one chose resentment over perseverance. We may not be responsible for what may have happened to us, but we are "response-able." We are responsible for how we handle and react to our challenges. We also have the power to control how our challenges affect us by our responses to them. For example, we have two people, who go through a very nasty divorce. One person faces their pain, owns it, learns from it and comes out better. But the other person is consumed by their pain, they can't move past the divorce, and so, become resentful towards everything in their life. Whichever way we choose has a big impact on our life. One response steals from us, and robs us of any growth or development we might gain from our challenges. While the other response gives us the opportunity to learn from our challenges, and become better people just for having experienced those challenges.

In life, facing challenges is a given. Jesus, himself, tells us that, but the good news is that Jesus "overcame the world," and so we, too, will overcome our challenges. We have the strength to overcome these trials. The power to overcome our trials lies within us. That's why it is very important that we learn how to overcome the challenges in our lives.

When you look closely, the word 'challenge' contains the word 'change.' Challenges aren't end points. Challenges are a change in our lives that push us forward. Challenges promote growth and valuable lessons. Challenges also offer a way for us to help others going through similar challenges like when Brene Brown says, "One day you will tell your story of how you overcame what you went through and it will be someone else's survival guide." Challenges also help us remain calm and focused under pressure because of what we have faced in the past, and that's a vital skill especially dealing with the ongoing Pandemic.

So, how do we overcome our challenges using Faith as a guide? Well, let's look at some tips and tools that can help!

Maintaining a Positive Mindset

Always remember this quote by Craig Groeschel, "Most of life's battles are either won or lost in our minds." The fight to overcome our challenge(s) starts in our minds. That is why it is crucial to maintain a positive mindset.

There are many benefits to having a positive mindset during a difficult trial of life. A positive mindset geared towards our outlook on life makes a lot of difference on the challenges we face. A positive mindset keeps you motivated and focused on overcoming any challenge that comes your way. A positive mindset encourages you to never give up. A positive mindset makes you hopeful. Above all, a positive mindset keeps away those negative energies that may try to pull you down. It changes your perspective, and a positive change in perspective is everything. A positive mindset is like when a light bulb turns on in your mind – that ah-ha moment when you're finally able to see through the dark. When that negative turns into a positive, you're already going to win.

Prayers and Meditation

Co-author, Connie Ajah-Ayang, speaking, "I personally use Faith, prayers, and meditation. Around the start of the pandemic, as I mentioned in my story, I became sick with every symptom in the book for Covid-19. I had to quarantine at home, while also isolating myself from my family. It was hard and difficult, especially for my kids. I couldn't even hug them. Who knew that hugs would be part of the things we took for granted during normal times? During those difficult two weeks, my prayers strengthened and sustained me.

After two weeks off, I returned to work. As I reached the parking lot, I sensed a fear taking hold of me. This fear spoke to me. It whispered, "You just got sick, and yet, you're going back in there? There are sick patients with coronavirus in there. What are you thinking? You are going to get sick again." I refused to give in to that fear. Instead, I listened to my Spirit. It whispered this scripture to me, "So do not fear, for I am with you; do not be dismayed, for I am your God. I will strengthen you and help you; I will uphold you with my righteous right hand." (Isaiah 41:10, NIV). As I repeated those words out loud to myself, I could feel a change in my spirit. Instantly, I had courage. I felt strengthened knowing that God was with me. My faith was strengthened. I *could* go back to work and serve. I *could* do what we are called to do. I *could* provide comfort and healing to our patients. With Faith, prayer and meditation, we can overcome our challenges.

For example, simply look at how God interacted with Elijah in 1 Kings 19:1-14 (NKJV). In this parable, God encourages a distraught and very discouraged Elijah, who flees to the wilderness in fear of his life. Elijah had executed some false prophets, and in retaliation, Jezebel wanted his life. In the wilderness, Elijah cries out to God. God steps in through a visitation from His angels to assist Elijah. When Elijah wants to give up, God steps in to not only protect him but also to provide for his physical needs. He has food to eat and water to drink. He was strengthened by God to continue his journey through the wilderness. This shows us that when we face challenges, we ought to remember that God will help us. As long as we pray to him, God will be there to help us. David even confirms this when he speaks in Psalm 121:1-2 (NIV), "I lift up my eyes to the mountains – where does my help come from? My help comes from the Lord, the Maker of heaven and earth." David knew that his God was bigger than the challenges he faced. He knew the healing and protective power of God would sustain him. All he had to do was pray.

Co-author, Gifty Boateng, states, "When I am stressed, praying and meditating help me to stay calm. Prayer and meditation are my rock during stressful moments. Prayer and meditation are my connection to my source of peace. Prayer is my way of getting my inner self into focus. When I feel myself getting overwhelmed by my responsibilities, I pray and meditate. Those two steps help to clear my mind and organize my thoughts. I stand firm in my prayers and meditation when the waves of uncertainty come my way. You, too, can stand firm in your prayers and meditation.

Co-author, Gifty Boateng, continues, "When I pray, I build up my faith. Just as scripture says, "...faith cometh by hearing, and hearing the word of God." (Romans 10:17, KJV). I speak to my Creator. I share all my fears, thoughts and feelings. After I pray, I sit in silence and meditate. I listen to the voice of peace that speaks to me in the stillness. When I meditate, I strengthen the core muscles of my being. When I meditate, I strengthen my mind against any negativity. Meditating keeps me from drowning in my fears and stresses, and reminds me that I am stronger than my negative thoughts. When I meditate, I think of things that are pure, lovely and blessed. The more I meditate on goodness – the more that goodness becomes a part of me. Whatever I set my mind on, I become; therefore, I think lofty thoughts. When I pray, I declare my dreams a reality. Prayer is an act of Faith. When I pray, I know that there is someone bigger than me who cares for me. I do not have to face the world alone. It is a joy to know that I do not have to figure out everything by myself! God's ears are ready to hear me when I call. All I have to do is quietly sit in prayer and meditate, and then I can speak to my Creator.

God's ears are ready and willing right now to hear you too! He cares very much for you, and everything that concerns you! In Isaiah 59:1 (NIV), scripture proclaims, "... nor his ear too dull to hear." God hears you! He sees everything you are going through! Listen to him, and you can make it through!

Avoid Comparison

Sometimes, we might ask ourselves, "What Ifs...?" What if so and so had this challenge? I bet they would handle it better. These thoughts are only beneficial if we're seeking outside sources for help and guidance, but if we're constantly thinking these "What If...?" thoughts then we're not practicing a positive mindset.

"Comparison," as Teddy Roosevelt said, "is the thief of joy!" Our "What if...?" questions can lead us to comparing ourselves to others and feeling "less than." When I spiral myself into "What if...?" questions, I quickly do a mental health check, so I don't fall into the "trap" of comparing myself to others. Next, I use my positive mindset to change "What ifs...? into "What Is..." I turn my focus to, "What is it that I have?" and then I list the people or things I'm grateful for in my life. At the end of the day, no matter our circumstances, there is always something or someone to be grateful for. We're able to overcome our challenges when we let go of the spiraling "What if...?" thoughts, and don't compare ourselves to others.

However, some of us still look at other people's lives and feel like life is unfair. We ask ourselves, "Why should they have that instead of me? Why should they flourish when I can't even get my head above water?" You feel like their blessings should be yours. You think that what God has for you was given to them. But remember, what God has for you is *only* for you and no one else. You can't have the life of someone else, and there's nothing anyone can do about that. Even identical twins can never be the same in life. Remember, you are unique – in your path and purpose. When you compare yourself to others, you only hinder your own progress. You plant seeds of jealousy and envy, instead of seeds of gratefulness. You should have a heart of gratitude – for what you do have and for where you are at. You can neither have nor live the life of someone else. What you need to understand is that you can never become someone else, even if you try to, and no one else can be you either. When you stop comparing your life to others, you will overcome your challenges and you will also accomplish great things in your life. So, instead of comparing yourself, be grateful. Appreciate what you have and where you are at in your life! Focus on your path.

Run *your* race and stay in *your* lane! Focus on you! Don't worry about anyone else!

Instead of worrying about everyone else, *focus* on you. If you knew where God was about to take you, you would stop complaining, crying, and being sad. Instead, you would learn to just praise God – for we know that "all things work together for good." (Romans 8:28, NKJV).

Using A.S.K.

It is true that overcoming challenges is a process. It takes time and practice to master the art of overcoming challenges – whether in the workplace, your personal life or in relationships. And it is hardly a one size fits all approach.

In addition to the previously discussed self-help tools, there is also the application of the acronym A.S.K. Let's talk about this three-step self-help guide that we use in overcoming our challenges. This has always come in handy for us, and we hope it helps you too.

A.S.K. stands for: A-Acknowledge that you have a challenge. S-Seek out help. K-Know that you are not alone in your challenges. A.S.K. is about acknowledging that we have a (new or old) challenge, acknowledging that we need to reach out and ask others for help, and acknowledging that we aren't alone in our struggles.

A-Acknowledge that you are facing a challenge. Acknowledging a challenge that you can't easily overcome is hard. Your first reaction will usually be going into a state of denial. You will think, "No, how can it be possible?" You will deny that your spouse is divorcing you, someone has passed away, or you've lost your (short-term or long-term) job. Once you are in a state of denial, it can be hard to leave that place. We'd rather shield ourselves from our challenge(s), and act as if the trial doesn't exist. We'd rather pretend and go about our everyday lives as if everything is going well.

Based on the Kübler-Ross model of the "Stages of Grief," when we suppress our feelings what we are doing is commonly referred to as, "Masking." When we "Mask," we are burying or "masking" our feelings which causes more harm than good. Our bottled-up feelings ultimately create a negative energy that consequently impact our (mental and physical) health, the people around us, and our general outlook on life. Co-author Connie Ajah-Ayang wants you to know that, "It is okay, and important that during your trials you feel your feelings. It is okay to cry, to scream, to be sad, and even to be angry. But remember, what you won't do is give up on yourself or on God!" Instead of "masking" your feelings, you will acknowledge what you are going through, feel your feelings, and then start developing a solution. Then, seek out help!

S-Seek out help as soon as possible! Don't be afraid to ask for help. Seeking out help doesn't mean that you're weak or not strong enough to face this challenge. We have got to understand that as humans we all need each other. It's okay to reach out to others and ask for help. It's okay to share those bottled-up feelings with others once you have acknowledged that you have a challenge. Charles Kettering said, "A problem shared is a problem half solved." And he's right! Once you share your feelings, you may see your challenge(s) in a whole new light and your new perspective may help you come up with solutions to your challenge(s). And then, maybe you could even help others who may one day face the same challenge as you.

You can also have people carry your sandbags. When work becomes overwhelming, we can seek out help and delegate our tasks to others who are willing to help carry our sandbags. In the nursing field, there are nursing assistants or nursing techs. Your patients are assigned to you, but that doesn't mean that you should try and do everything by yourself. You don't need to carry your sandbag alone, especially on those hard shifts. You shouldn't think that you must be the only one to do everything about your patient care. There will be days when you can't catch up on your patient load, and those are the days when you should delegate your work to others before you get overwhelmed and stuck. When you delegate your work, you have time to brief, regroup and reprioritize your work. You'll then be able to focus on the higher priority things for your patients, learn time management and build trust amongst you and your co-workers.

There are also several other ways you can seek out help, such as, through friends, family, therapy, support groups and online resources. Finally, know that you are not alone.

K-Know that you are not alone in your challenge(s). We're all unique individuals, but most of the challenges we face aren't unique to us. We may handle our trials differently, but the bottom line is that there's always someone who has gone through the same thing or who is going through the same thing as us.

When you know that you're not alone in your struggle(s), you instantly have a sense of comfort and anxiety relief. As nurses, most of us have faced similar challenges during the outbreak of the pandemic. Many of us have never seen so many patients die on the job as much as we have seen during the pandemic's various surges. Many of us with school-age kids have had the same challenge of juggling our work and home lives while also keeping our kids focused on their virtual classes. It wasn't like that before when we were pre-pandemic. Now, we can't just put our kids on the bus and send them off to school as we go to work. Instead, we have to make sure our kids are safe at home and attending their online classes while we're at work.

Co-author, Connie Ajah-Ayang, recalls when she would sometimes receive a call from her six-year-old son's teacher while at work. "The teacher told me that he would leave his zoom class before he had been dismissed. I would then have to call my husband, who was at home sleeping because he worked nights, to check up on our boys. It was tough, and it still is, but knowing that I could talk to my fellow nurses, and learn from them and share ideas has been invaluable!

Connie Ajah-Ayang continues, "One day, I posted a question on my Facebook page about my challenges of working 8:30am-4:30pm, and not being able to be home with my kids to keep them focused on their virtual learning. I hoped that others with a similar challenge as me would share their thoughts, and boy was I right! I got a lot of different thoughts from other nurses and parents on what was working and what wasn't working for them." So, always remember that you are not alone in the challenge or trial you're facing.

Final Advice

Some days, you must remember to breathe and have Faith that everything will be okay! Know that God is greater than our obstacles. Understand that God is greater than our needs. God is greater than all our problems, and He can turn our situation(s) around! Yes, the challenge that you're currently facing shall pass, and you will come out stronger than before!

Yes, you can trust God with your life!

We are constantly fighting with ourselves or our subconscious/intrusive thoughts. We are constantly fighting about God's Truths about us, what the devil claims to "know" are truths about us, and about what we know are truths about us. However, we have the power to discern these truths from lies. When we meditate on the Word of God, we constantly remind ourselves of His promises and maintain a positive mindset on life. #TrustGodwithyourlife #Staypositive

Chapter Reflection:

When things go wrong, I typically...?

CHAPTER 5:

REMEMBERING GOD'S PROMISES

As the pandemic rages on, you can tell that we're all still currently adjusting to living in a 'new normal.' When you look around, you can see that our world is filled with instability and uncertainty. Every day seems to bring either disheartening news or new unanswered questions about Covid-19. And as a result of the mass confusion and mass grief, we've started asking the question, "How do we hold on to hope?" The simple and quick answer to that question is to, "focus your eyes on only Jesus." Yes, Jesus is the answer.

At any given time, we can choose to walk in fear or to walk in Faith. In this world, there are so many variables that would try to counteract our Faith, but we must choose to remain steadfast in our Faith. We need to stay in that *faith lane*. We need to see God work for us and through us. The reality of who God is to us and what He can and will do for us should always override and take precedence over what we see with our naked eyes. God works in unseen ways. Sickness, disease, loss of life, loss of property or losing a job are all realities of our lives, but God and His Words reach out to us through these hardships, and guide us to a clear path. God remains God. He is always a healer, helper and teacher. You must rely on God.

In 2 Timothy 1:7 (NKJV), scripture proclaims, "For God has not given us a spirit of fear, but of power and of love and of a sound mind!" Fear is one of those emotions that limits us and hinders our growth. And the truth is, *faith and fear cannot co-exist.* We need to grow more in our faith to conquer our fears. And as scripture proclaims, we have been given the "spirit of boldness and not fear," So, what are you afraid of? God has promised us boldness, love and a sound mind. Claim this promise today, and make it manifest in your life.

In Isaiah 41:10 (NKJV), the Lord proclaims, "Fear not, for I am with you; Be not dismayed, for I am your God. I will strengthen you, Yes, I will help you, I will uphold you with My righteous right hand." No matter what's going on in your life or in the world, remember that God is more powerful. Remember that the bible is full of many promises that God has made to us. God's promises are beneficial to us, so long as we believe in Him and have Faith in Him.

In Deuteronomy 31:8 (NIV), scripture proclaims, "The Lord himself goes before you and will be with you; he will never leave you nor forsake you. Do not be afraid; do not be discouraged." Sometimes, it becomes a little hard to believe that God really loves you or even cares for you when things are going wrong. But He does! Remember, God never promised us that life would be without challenges or that life would be easy. Instead, He promised us that if we stayed in Faith then He would take what was meant to harm us and use it for our benefit. He promised us that he would give us a peace that surpasses all human understanding. As nurses, we want to be able to remember these promises from God. Even though God doesn't always give us everything we want, He does always fulfill His promises to us. He leads us along the way to the safest paths to Himself and His Truths.

In Romans 8:28 (NIV), scripture proclaims, "And we know that in all things God works for the good of those who love him, who have been called according to his purpose." God has a purpose for your life. The struggles you're facing today are preparing you with the strength that you'll need to get through tomorrow. In your struggles, remember to see your purpose. Remember that, there is a purpose for pain, for loss, for tragedy and for suffering. So, instead of asking, "God, why me? God, why is this happening? God, where are you?" Ask instead, "God, what do you need me to learn from this? What lesson do you, Lord, want me to get out of this pain and suffering?"

In Psalm 32:8 (NIV), scripture proclaims, "I will instruct you and teach you in the way you should go; I will counsel you with my loving eye on you."

In Matthew 11:28 (NIV), Matthew proclaims, "Come to me, all you who are weary and burdened, and I will give you rest."

In 2 Corinthians 12:9 (NIV), scripture proclaims, "But he said to me, 'My grace is sufficient for you, for my power is made perfect in weakness.' Therefore, I will boast all the more gladly about my weaknesses, so that Christ's power may rest on me."

In Isaiah 40:31 (NIV), scripture proclaims "...but those who hope in the Lord will renew their strength. They will soar on wings like eagles; they will run and not grow weary, they will walk and not be faint."

In Jeremiah 29:11 (NIV), scripture proclaims, "For I know the plans I have for you," declares the Lord, "plans to prosper you and not to harm you, plans to give you hope and a future."

In Psalm 34:4 (NIV), scripture proclaims, "I sought the Lord, and he answered me; he delivered me from all my fears."

In Psalm 34:18 (NIV), scripture proclaims, "The Lord is close to the brokenhearted and saves those who are crushed in spirit."

In Philippians 4:6-9 (NIV), scripture proclaims, "Do not be anxious about anything, but in every situation, by prayer and petition, with thanksgiving, present your requests to God. And the peace of God, which transcends all understanding, will guard your hearts and your minds in Christ Jesus. Finally, brothers and sisters, whatever is true, whatever is noble, whatever is right, whatever is pure, whatever is lovely, whatever is admirable – if anything is excellent or praiseworthy – think about such things. Whatever you have learned or received or heard from me or seen in me – put it into practice. And the God of peace will be with you."

In Isaiah 43:2 (NIV), scripture proclaims, "When you pass through the waters, I will be with you; and when you pass through the rivers, they will not sweep over you. When you walk through the fire, you will not be burned; the flames will not set you ablaze."

In Isaiah 61:1 (NIV), scripture proclaims, "The Spirit of the Sovereign LORD is on me, because the LORD has anointed me to proclaim good news to the poor. He has sent me to bind up the brokenhearted, to proclaim freedom for the captives and release from darkness for the prisoners..."

In Colossians 3:23 (NIV), scripture proclaims, "Whatever you do, work at it with all your heart, as working for the Lord, not for human masters."

In Philippians 4:13 (NIV), scripture proclaims, "I can do all this through him who gives me strength. Let's be real, there are some days when you can't even get out of bed. You feel so overwhelmed and tired of everything that's going on. But instead of throwing in the towel, it is on those days of weariness that we must draw form God's promises. This scripture verse reminds us of the fact that with our Faith in God and belief in ourselves we *can do All things through Christ* who empowers us.

In Psalm 118:6 (NIV), scripture proclaims, "The LORD is with me; I will not be afraid. What can mere mortals do to me?"

In 1 Peter 5:7 (NIV), scripture proclaims, "Cast all your anxiety on him because he cares for you." Remember to always bring your worries to God. Talk to Him in your times of distress just as scripture reminds us to do.

In 2 Chronicles 15:7 (NIV), scripture proclaims, "But as for you, be strong and do not give up, for your work will be rewarded."

In Matthew 5:13-16 (NIV), Matthew proclaims, "You are the salt of the earth. But if the salt loses its saltiness, how can it be made salty again? It is no longer good for anything, except to be thrown out and trampled underfoot. You are the light of the world. A town built on a hill cannot be hidden. Neither do people light a lamp and put it under a bowl. Instead they put it on its stand, and it gives light to everyone in the house. In the same way, let your light shine before others, that they may see your good deeds and glorify your Father in heaven."

In 1 Corinthians 15:58 (NIV), scripture proclaims, "Therefore, my dear brothers and sisters, stand firm. Let nothing move you. Always give yourselves fully to the work of the Lord, because you know that your labor in the Lord is not in vain."

In Psalm 18:32 (NIV), scripture proclaims, "It is God who arms me with strength and keeps my way secure." God gives us the strength to carry on. He sustains us as He promised he would.

In 1 Corinthians 2:5 (NIV), scripture proclaims, "...your faith might not rest on human wisdom, but on God's power.

In Ephesians 2:10 (NIV), scripture proclaims, "For we are God's hand-iwork, created in Christ Jesus to do good works, which God prepared in advance for us to do." Remember that God is our provider. He is capable of providing for us – more than we can even imagine. As far as you can think or even imagine, God is *able* and *willing* to do it for you. In Ephesians 3:20 (NIV), scripture proclaims, "Now to him who is able to do immeasurably more than all we ask or imagine, according to his power that is at work within us." There is nothing that we desire that God cannot provide. This scripture reminds us that as far as we can imagine it God is not only able, but also willing to provide that which we may not even think of ourselves. So, hold on to his promises in your times of need.

In Ephesians 6:10 (NIV), scripture proclaims, "Finally, be strong in the Lord and in his mighty power."

In Deuteronomy 31:6 (NIV), scripture proclaims, "Be strong and courageous. Do not be afraid or terrified because of them, for the Lord your God goes with you; he will never leave you nor forsake you."

In Philippians 1:6 (NIV), scripture proclaims, "...being confident of this, that he who began a good work in you will carry it on to completion until the day of Christ Jesus."

In Galatians 6:9 (NIV), scripture proclaims, "Let us not become weary in doing good, for at the proper time we will reap a harvest if we do not give up."

In 1 Corinthians 9:24 (NIV), scripture proclaims, "Do you not know that in a race all the runners run, but only one gets the prize? Run in such a way as to get the prize."

In Psalm 28:7 (NIV), scripture proclaims, "The Lord is my strength and my shield; my heart trusts in him, and he helps me. My heart leaps for joy, and with my song I praise him."

In Psalm 3:3 (NIV), scripture proclaims, "But You, Lord, are a shield around me, my glory, the One who lifts my head high."

In Isaiah 41:10 (NIV), scripture proclaims, "So do not fear, for I am with you; do not be dismayed for I am your God. I will strengthen you and help you; I will uphold you with my righteous right hand." Sometimes, we may feel lonely. We may feel like we are all alone in our struggles. But you need to remember this: God is Always present. This scripture and the promise from God are a reminder to us that God is Omnipresent. He will always be present. He will strengthen us. He will help us. He will sustain us. When we feel lonely and helpless, we can take refuge in God. Do not fear! You are not alone!

In Psalm 46:1 (NIV), scripture proclaims, "God is our refuge and strength, an ever-present help in trouble." When in doubt, always remember that you can completely trust in God. We can always trust God, instead; of relying on our own understanding, wisdom or knowledge because God knows all. In Proverbs 3:5-6 (NIV), scripture proclaims, "Trust in the Lord with all your heart and lean not on your own understanding; in all your ways submit to him and he will make your paths straight." When we trust in Him to direct us daily, we are sure to walk in His purpose.

In John 1:2 (NIV), John proclaims, "He was with God in the beginning."

In 3 John 1:2 (NIV), John proclaims, "Dear friend, I pray that you may enjoy good health and that all may go well with you, even as your soul is getting along well."

In Matthew 28:20 (NIV), Matthew proclaims, "...And surely, I am with you always, to the very end of the age."

In Jeremiah 33:3 (NIV), scripture proclaims, "Call to me and I will answer you and tell you great and unsearchable things you do not know."

In Deuteronomy 7:9 (NIV), scripture proclaims, "Know therefore that the Lord your God is God; he is the faithful God, keeping his covenant of love to a thousand generations of those who love him and keep his commandments."

In Genesis 50:20 (NIV), scripture proclaims, "You intended to harm me, but God intended it for good to accomplish what is now being done, the saving of many lives.

In Jeremiah 17:7 (NIV), scripture proclaims, "But blessed is the one who trusts in the Lord, whose confidence is in him."

In 1 Chronicles 16:34 (NIV), scripture proclaims, "Give thanks to the Lord, for he is good; his love endures forever."

In Psalm 23:1 (NIV), scripture proclaims, "The Lord is my shepherd, I lack nothing."

In Psalm 23:4 (NIV), scripture proclaims, "Even though I walk through the darkest valley, I will fear no evil, for you are with me; your rod and your staff, they comfort me."

In Psalm 46:1 (NIV), scripture proclaims, "God is our refuge and strength, an ever-present help in trouble."

In Psalm 18:2 (NIV), scripture proclaims, "The Lord is my rock, my fortress and my deliverer; my God is my rock, in whom I take refuge, my shield and the horn of my salvation, my stronghold."

In Psalm 27:13 (NIV), scripture proclaims, "I remain confident of this: I will see the goodness of the Lord in the land of the living."

In Psalm 94:19 (NIV), scripture proclaims, "When anxiety was great within me, your consolation brought me joy."

In Matthew 19:26 (NIV), Matthew proclaims, "Jesus looked at them and said, 'With man this is impossible, but with God all things are possible.'

In Romans 8:31 (NIV), scripture proclaims, "What, then, shall we say in response to these things? If God is for us, who can be against us?"

In Psalm 118:24 (NKJV), scripture proclaims, "This is the day the Lord has made; We will rejoice and be glad in it."

In Galatians 5:22-23 (NKJV), scripture proclaims, "But the fruit of the Spirit is love, joy, peace, forbearance, kindness, goodness, faithfulness, gentleness, and self-control." Joy – as we all know – is a very contagious feeling, so much so, that even musician, Carlos Santana, has said, "If you carry joy in your heart, you can heal any moment." When we care for our patients, we cannot underestimate the power of our smiles. We should exude joy and brighten up a patient's day. In Proverbs 17:22 (NIV), scripture proclaims, "A cheerful heart is good medicine, but a crushed spirit dries up the bones." Our smiles are medicinal, and can have a healing effect on our patients.

Remember who you are and whose you are. You are from God, and loved by Him more than you may ever know. During life's chaos, we are fearful, but despite the struggles remember that God is with you. God is always with you. Remember that your faith is unshakable. Your hope can be anchored. Your future is secured. Why? Because your Heavenly Father dearly loves you, and His heart is blessing you! He wants the best for you. He gives us His grace and mercy for what we face today, and then He gives us His Faith and hope for what we may encounter tomorrow. When we need Him, God will be there for us. He will meet us in those places of desperation, hopelessness and despair. His promises will always pull us out of the trenches of fear and panic. In our moments of weakness, He will deliver His strength to us. He will bring us peace during the storm. In the moments when we are hurting, overwhelmed or afraid, we need to remember His Words and declare His promises over our lives and our circumstances.

In James 1:2 (NKJV), the apostle James proclaims, "...count it all joy when you fall into various trials..." He doesn't say that because he enjoys the "various trials" he goes through. He says that because he knows that

God has him, and will see him through these trials. He continues in James 1:3 (NKJV), "...knowing that the testing of your faith produces patience." So, our trials build us up. They help us develop our *faith muscles.* James knows we serve and worship a God, who is with us and for us – against it all! Yes, we serve a God, who is bigger than all our challenges combined. There is no one greater than our God. Whenever you feel like life is weighing you down, please, get on your knees and pray. He is there! Whenever you feel like life is too hard, activate your faith by meditating on God's promises. He is there! He will never fail!

Chapter Reflection:

Which of God's promises are you standing on in this season?

CHAPTER 6:

DAILY DOSE OF INSPIRATION: FAITH AF-FIRMATIONS

As nurses, we are called to encourage, to help, to inspire and to give hope to others, but most times we need that encouragement reciprocated back to us, especially during this pandemic. Nurses – just like the medication doses we administer – need a 'daily dose of Inspiration' to keep us motivated and inspired, so that, we never give up despite the challenges!

Giving up is not an option. Giving up on our patients that rely on us in these challenging and uncertain times is not an option!

Our Words!

Faith's Confessions Create Realities. It's known that when you whole-heartedly believe in God's words with Faith, and speak about His Words aloud that their positive effects on your life manifest themselves. It has been long established that when you believe in your heart and confess with your mouth, then His Words will become real to you. Affirming positive affirmations about yourself and your Faith is one way of bolstering up your spirit as you begin your day. These are brief statements that you can say aloud to help restructure your mindset.

The words you speak identify you. The words you speak set the boundaries for your life. The words you speak affect your Spirit. Our words are very powerful, and have a significant effect on us and others. In Proverbs 18:21 (NIV), the scripture proclaims, "The tongue has the power of life and death, and those who love it will eat its fruit." Our words can speak either life or death. Our words can either build others up or tear them down. That is why we should be careful about what we say about ourselves and others. Our intrusive thoughts, or the devil can make us believe in all the lies about ourselves. These lies slip in at our weakest spots. They hurl cruel things at us like, "How we can't make it. We're not good enough. We'll never be great nurses. Etc." During those times, we must remember that we've got the power to challenge that narrative. We've got the power to counteract these lies with our positive affirmations about who we *really* are. We can change our perspective from a negative mindset to a positive mindset. When lies say you can't do it, you tell them, "Oh, you liars! I Can and I Will!" When they claim you're not good enough, you tell them, "I Am More than Enough."

As stated above, the words you speak identify you. The words you speak set the boundaries for your life. The words you speak affect your Spirit. And if you don't truly think before you speak, then you won't understand that *you will never realize much beyond the words you speak into your life.* You are what you say. You will have what you say, so think before you speak!

Our Thoughts!

The greatest prison we can ever find ourselves in is in our own thoughts.

Co-author, Connie Ajah-Ayang, suggests, "Before you start your shift at work, try starting with a positive mindset! Try telling yourself, 'I *deserve* to have a good day! I am *worth* having a good day at work today!'" She continues, "Positive thoughts breed positive energy, and great outcomes too. Try to think of some inspiring words. Whether said by you or someone else, inspiring words still have the same effect on us. They can truly brighten our day and uplift our spirits. At the end of this chapter, we challenge you to create a list of daily affirmations of your own to speak to yourself. These must be words or phrases to live by or that will inspire you or both. You must be assured that these words will become your reality. We hope these quotes and affirmations get you inspired and are helpful to you!

Inspirational Quotes:

"Where the needs of the world and your talents cross, there lies your vocation."—Aristotle

"You are not here merely to make a living. You are here in order to enable the world to live more amply, with greater vision, with a finer spirit of hope and achievement. You are here to enrich the world, and you impoverish yourself if you forget the errand."—Woodrow Wilson

"Too often we underestimate the power of a touch, a smile, a kind word, a listening ear, an honest compliment, or the smallest act of caring, all of which have the potential to turn a life around."—Leo Buscaglia

"CARING is the essence of NURSING."—Jean Watson

"Bound by paperwork, short on hands, sleep, and energy...nurses are rarely short on caring."—Sharon Hudacek

"There are two ways to live your life. One is as though nothing is a miracle. The other is as though everything is a miracle."—Albert Einstein

"A problem is a chance for you to do your best."—Duke Ellington

"Your work is going to fill a large part of your life, and the only way to be truly satisfied is to do what you believe is great work. And the only way to do great work is to love what you do."–Steve Jobs

"Never give up on a dream just because of the time it will take to accomplish it. The time will pass anyway."–Earl Nightingale

"When you're a nurse you know that every day you will touch a life or a life will touch yours."–Anonymous

"Every challenge or trial you are going through now is preparing you, and developing the strength muscles you will need for tomorrow."–Connie Ajah-Ayang

"If you can't figure out your purpose, figure out your passion. For passion will lead you right into your purpose."–Bishop T.D. Jakes

"Every nurse is an angel with a key for a healthy community! All in caring for patients is part of the nursing soul."–Aleksandar Radunovic

"Your profession is not what brings home your weekly paycheck, your profession is what you're put on earth to do, with such passion and such intensity that it becomes spiritual in calling."–Vincent Van Gogh

"If you let the closed door discourage you, you will not be ready for the blessings of the open doors."–Connie Ajah-Ayang

"If you don't step out of your comfort zone, you will not grow! You can't keep doing the same thing over and over and expect different results."–Connie Ajah-Ayang

"The trained nurse has become one of the great blessings of humanity, taking a place beside the physician and the priest, and not inferior to either in her mission."–William Osler

"Sometimes I inspire my patients; more often they inspire me."–Anonymous

"Nurses dispense comfort, compassion, and caring without even a prescription."—Val Saintsbury

"Nursing is one of the Fine Arts: I had almost said, the finest of Fine Arts."—Florence Nightingale

"To do what nobody else will do, a way that nobody else can do, in spite of all we go through; that is to be a NURSE."—Rawsi Williams

"I'm not telling you it is going to be easy – I'm telling you it's going to be worth it."—Art Williams

"A nurse is compassion in SCRUBS."—Lexie Saige

"Our job as nurses is to cushion the sorrow and celebrate the joy, everyday, while we are 'just doing our jobs.'"—Christine Belle, RN, BSN

"Nurses don't wait until October to celebrate 'Make a Difference Day' – they make a difference every day!"—Anonymous

"The character of the nurse is as important as the knowledge she possesses."—Carolyn Jarvis

"As we let our own light shine, we unconsciously give other people permission to do the same."—Nelson Mandela

"Kindness is the language which the deaf can hear and the blind can see."—Mark Twain

"To know even one life has breathed easier because you have lived. This is to have succeeded."—Ralph Waldo Emerson

"When you have done EVERYTHING, sometimes the only thing left to do is pray. Get Out of Your Own Way!"—Connie Ajah-Ayang

"Our minds have been made to create both negative and positive thoughts, but it is the one you give attention to that has the power over your life."—Connie Ajah-Ayang and Gifty Boateng

"Sometimes, the only way to 'get through' a challenge or trial is to 'go through,' and that is called Endurance!"–Connie Ajah-Ayang

"No condition is hopeless so long as it involves God, and no condition is Helpless so long as it involves God. He is our ever-present help in our time of need."–Connie Ajah-Ayang

"As a nurse, we have the opportunity to heal the mind, soul, heart, and body of our patients, their families, and ourselves. They may forget your name, but they will never forget how you made them feel."–Maya Angelou

"The best way to find yourself is to lose yourself in the service of others."–Mahatma Ghandi

"Being a nurse means to hold all your own tears and start drawing smiles on people's faces. Nursing is sacrificing."–Dana Basem

"Success is not final, failure is not fatal: it is the courage to continue that counts."–Winston Churchill

"A nurse will always give us hope, an angel with a stethoscope."–Carrie Latet

"No matter how difficult the days may get, never forget the reason you became a nurse."–Anonymous

"Worrying is like a rocking chair: it gives you something to do but never gets you anywhere."–Erma Bombeck

"I attribute my success to this – I never gave or took any excuse."–Florence Nightingale

"I think one's feelings waste themselves in words; they ought all to be distilled into actions which bring results."–Florence Nightingale

"Always place God in front of your Day/Shift, allow him to lead your work for his glory–Gifty Boateng

"There are gifts inside of you. Manifest these gifts to your patients and families through gifts of compassion, caring, kindness, empathy, and more."–Gifty Boateng

"Take control of your mind or it will control you."–Connie Ajah-Ayang

"As a nurse, never underestimate the healing effects of your smile on your patient."–Connie Ajah-Ayang

"God's plan for you is greater than any plan you can think of."–Steve Harvey

"If you want to be successful you have to jump, there's no way around it. If you're safe, you'll never soar."–Steve Harvey

"It is one thing to pray. It is another thing when you believe as you pray – and that is Faith."–Connie Ajah-Ayang.

"You have to aspire to something so great that you have to have God's help."–Steve Harvey

"Even when you don't have the energy to put your prayers into words, trust that God hears the murmurs of your heart."–Connie Ajah-Ayang

"Failure is a great teacher, and I think when you make mistakes and you recover from them and you treat them as valuable learning experiences, then you've got something to share."–Steve Harvey

"Sometimes, on your very worst shifts you don't have to think, wonder or obsess over everything that could've, would've, or should've. You just have to breathe and have faith that everything will work out well in the end."–Connie Ajah-Ayang

"The 4 P's to success: pressure, persistence, perseverance & prayer."–Steve Harvey

"Wake up and smile! Wake up and be grateful!"–Steve Harvey

"Catch fire today! Make today the day you stop complaining and do something."–Steve Harvey

"What you want out of life is the thing you have to give the most of."–Steve Harvey

"Do not ignore the passion that burns in you. Spend time to discover your gift."–Steve Harvey

"When you're up in life, your friends get to know who you are. When you're down in life, you get to know who your friends are."–Steve Harvey

"Smile, not because everything is going well in your life or because everything is perfect. No, smile just because you are Alive! That by itself is a blessing."–Connie Ajah-Ayang

"Your dream has to be bigger than your fear."–Steve Harvey

"You can never be someone else, even if you try to. So don't try to follow the crowd. Be authentic. Be 'unapologetically you.' Be you! You are Unique."–Connie Ajah-Ayang

"Tired? Don't Give Up. God Knows. God Sees. God Hears. God Cares. Breathe and Relax."–Connie Ajah-Ayang

"Don't wish it were easier, wish you were better. Don't wish for fewer problems, wish for more skills. Don't wish for less challenges, wish for more wisdom."–Earl Shoaf

"A caress, a smile, is full of meaning for one who is sick. It is a simple gesture, but encouraging, he or she feels accompanied, feels closer to being healed, feels like a person, not a number."–Pope Francis

"Nurses are always there, you care for us from the earliest years. You look after us in our happiest and saddest times. And for many, you look after us and our families at the end of our lives. Your dedication and professionalism are awe-inspiring."—Duchess Kate Middleton

"Let us never consider ourselves finished nurses...we must be learning all of our lives."— Florence Nightingale

"I think the greatest obstacle to our full potential is the fear of failing and not failing to try."—Connie Ajah-Ayang

"The most important practical lesson that can be given to nurses is to teach them what to observe."—Florence Nightingale

"Nursing is a progressive art such that to stand still is to go backwards."—Florence Nightingale

"No one is going to walk into your life and Change it. Look in the mirror. You alone have the power to change your life. Stop waiting and start acting."—Connie Ajah-Ayang

"Rather than focusing on how big the problem is, focus on how big God is and Trust Him."—Connie Ajah-Ayang

"If a nurse declines to do these kinds of things for her patient, 'because it is not her business,' I should say that nursing was not her calling. I have seen surgical sisters, women whose hands were worth to them two or three guineas a-week, down upon their knees scouring a room or hut, because they thought it otherwise not fit for their patients to go into. I am far from wishing nurses to scour. It is a waste of power. But I do say that these women had the true nurse-calling – the good of their sick first, and second only the consideration what it was their 'place' to do – and that women who wait for the housemaid to do this, or for the charwoman to do that, when their patients are suffering, have not the making of a nurse in them."—Florence Nightingale

"If you must grow, be willing to push past your limitations. Be willing to push past the familiarity that is where growth begins."–Connie Ajah-Ayang

"If you wait to do everything until you're sure it's right, you'll probably never do much of anything."–Win Borden

"The nurse is temporarily the consciousness of the unconscious, the love of life of the suicidal, the leg of the amputee, the eyes of the newly blind, a means of locomotion for the newborn, knowledge and confidence for the young mother, a voice for those too weak to speak, and so on."–Virginia Henderson, RN

"Trust yourself. You know more than you think you do." –Benjamin Spock

"Confidence is not 'they will like me.' Confidence is 'I'll be fine if they don't.'"–Christina Grimmie

"Successful people have fear, successful people have doubts, and successful people have worries. They just don't let these feelings stop them."–T. Harv Eker

"Forgive yourself, you are not perfect. Show yourself grace. You are still learning. Show yourself patience. You are on a journey."–Anonymous

"Every nurse was drawn to nursing because of a desire to care, to serve, or to help."–Christina Feist-Heilmeier, RN

"When I think about all the patients and their loved ones that I have worked with over the years, I know most of them don't remember me nor I them. But I do know that I gave a little piece of myself to each of them and they to me and those threads make up the beautiful tapestry in my mind that is my career in nursing."–Donna Wilk Cardillo

"To know even one life has breathed easier because you have lived. This is to have succeeded."–Ralph Waldo Emerson

"Be the nurse you would want as a patient"–Anonymous

"America's nurses are the beating heart of our medical system."–Barack Obama

"You treat a disease: you win, you lose. You treat a person: I guarantee you win, you'll win, no matter the outcome."–Robin Williams

"Let no one ever come to you without leaving better and happier."–Mother Teresa

"Not all angels have wings...some have scrubs."–Anonymous

"Apprehension, uncertainty, waiting, expectation, fear of surprise, do a patient more harm than any exertion."–Florence Nightingale

"Life is not easy for any of us. But what of that? We must have perseverance and above all confidence in ourselves. We must believe that we are gifted for something, and that this thing, at whatever cost, must be attained."–Marie Curie

"It's not what you know or who you know. It's what you are that finally counts."–Zig Ziglar

"Keep your thoughts positive because your thoughts become your words. Keep your words positive because your words become your behavior. Keep your behavior positive because your behavior becomes your habits. Keep your habits positive because your habits become your values. Keep your values positive because your values become your destiny."–Mahatma Gandhi

"What do we live for, if it is not to make life less difficult for each other?"–Mary Ann Evans

"If you'll not settle for anything less than your best, you will be amazed at what you can accomplish in your lives."–Vince Lombardi

"People often say that motivation doesn't last. Well, neither does bathing – that's why we recommend it daily."–Zig Ziglar

"To accomplish great things, we must not only act, but also dream; not only plan, but also believe."–Anatole France

"Cooperation is the thorough conviction that nobody can get there unless everybody gets there."–Virginia Burden Tower

"When God allows you to go through pain, just know that there's a purpose for that pain. Hang tight. Don't quit on yourself or God. Because if you know the purpose, you will endure the process and once you endure the process, you will enjoy the product. So, don't give up. Someday you are going to look back at all the progress you have made and be glad you didn't quit!"–Connie Ajah-Ayang

Daily Affirmations: An affirmation is the act of confirming and believing something to be true. Positive affirmations or positive self-talk has become a popular phenomenon to help inspire confidence in children and in adults too. It helps restructure one's mindset from negative thoughts to positive thoughts. These positive statements or affirmations become our reality. The power with affirmations just like with Faith is that if they're not said with a strong conviction then they are only words.

Co-author, Connie Ajah-Ayang, recalls a conversation she had with her youngest son. "He said something like, 'I'm a tough guy.' And so, I asked him what it meant to be a 'tough guy.' He then listed that he "was strong and smart. He could be anything he wanted, and that he knew everything." I was impressed. I realized my son had just stated his affirmations. I was so proud of him for having such confidence and for believing in his abilities. That is what he believes, and no one can tell him differently. Those were *his* affirmations."

Affirmations help us get through our rough days by believing in the positive thoughts, assertions and statements we daily tell ourselves. According to the Nurse & Midwife support article, "positive self-talk in the form of Affirmations can lead to improved self-esteem, controlled stress management, enhanced well-being, and a reduced impact of depression, anxiety and other personality disorders." (Holland 2018). And did you know that repeating the same affirmation three times makes a lot more of a difference than only saying it once? Affirmations can have a lasting impact on how you feel, and what you do next. Try these daily affirmations out for yourself. We hope they help brighten your day!

"Today is the day the Lord has made. I choose to be joyful and put the devil to shame."–Connie Ajah-Ayang

"I chose nursing to let my light shine before all my patients."–Gifty Boateng

"My hands and my head are anointed with oil and my cup runneth over for my patients."–Gifty Boateng

"The time is N.O.W. – Nurses Overcoming and Winning!"–Gifty Boateng

"No matter what I face at work, I know who I am and whose I am."–Connie Ajah-Ayang

"God has given me the mantle of Grit and Resilience."–Gifty Boateng

"Nothing will get in my way this week."–Connie Ajah-Ayang

"I'm ONLY influenced by the WORD of God!"–Gifty Boateng

"I became a nurse to make an Impact."–Gifty Boateng

"Today is a good day to do great things for my patients and for myself."–Connie Ajah-Ayang

"I am confident in my clinical judgment skills to provide excellent care."—Connie Ajah-Ayang

"I am confident in my abilities in caring for my patients."—Gifty Boateng

I am a nurse; nursing is what I do.

I Am Confident in who I Am and my Abilities.

I have the clarity of mind to make good moral judgment concerning my patients.

"Instead of thinking I can't, I choose to think I can, and I will!"—Connie Ajah-Ayang

"I am focused and cannot be distracted from my goals!"—Connie Ajah-Ayang

I am strong in mind, body and spirit.

Stop telling yourself that you are not good enough, instead; try this: I Am worthy, and I Am More than Enough!

I became a nurse to make a difference, and that is what I do.

If I can't change it, I will let it go.

It's okay if I have to cry. It's okay if I have to scream. But what I will not do is give up!

I didn't come this far to just up and quit. No, quitting is not an option.

I will continue to grow, learn and gain new knowledge.

"I am determined, motivated and dedicated to my job."—Gifty Boateng

"I believe in the person I want to become!"—Connie Ajah-Ayang

"Today, I have total control of my thoughts and my mind!"–Connie Ajah-Ayang

"I choose Faith over fear Every day!"–Gifty Boateng

"I am claiming Abundance. I am Claiming Peace, Love, Happiness and all-round Success!"–Connie Ajah-Ayang

"I am intentional in everything I do!"–Connie Ajah-Ayang

"I am loved, blessed and cannot be stressed about anything."–Gifty Boateng

Today, I choose Worship over Worry."–Connie Ajah-Ayang

I keep my mind right, my body tight and I work hard.

"What God has for me is for me and there's nothing anyone can do about it!"–Connie Ajah-Ayang

"I am blessed to be a blessing to others."–Gifty Boateng

I work hard and pray even harder.

"I still believe, despite what I may go through, I Still Believe."–Connie Ajah-Ayang

I am the best at what I do.

I can do this, and it will not break me.

I am born a winner.

I don't chase. I attract, and what belongs to me will always find me.

"I choose to Trust God no matter what happens today during my shift."–Gifty Boateng

"Today is a new day. I am open to new possibilities for myself and my patients."–Gifty Boateng

God is always with me!

"I choose to be free of hurt, anger, and hatred."–Connie Ajah-Ayang

"I choose to let go of fear and doubt towards my career goals and in being of service to my patients."–Gifty Boateng

"Nothing will be impossible for me because I am in Christ, and through him, I can do all things."–Connie Ajah-Ayang

"I Am Completely Forgiven, and I am free of all guilt."–Connie Ajah-Ayang

I may not be Perfect; I make mistakes and that is completely okay!

"With God by my side, I Am Unstoppable."–Gifty Boateng

I will not look back.

I will not hold back.

"I will not be held back, and by all means I will keep Moving Forward."–Connie Ajah-Ayang

I choose to see the Good in Everyone.

"Today, I refuse to listen to the voice of discouragement, fear and rejection. I choose to allow the Word of God to be the loudest voice I hear."–Connie Ajah-Ayang

I Will Not give up on who I Am becoming – no matter what.

"My current situation is not my last destination. This too shall pass."–Connie Ajah-Ayang

I am firmly rooted, built up, established in my Faith and overflowing with gratitude.

Today and every day, I will fill my mind with positive thoughts.

Everything is getting better every day. I have survived worst days and there are better days ahead.

I have so much to be grateful for.

I always try to see the good in people, even when it gets tough.

Today, I made my mind up. I will press past all the anger and bitterness. I will be a blessing wherever I go.

You are unique all the way through so make it count!

Smiling can literally improve your mood, and fool your brain into being happy.

The mind is a powerful tool, so use it to send some affirmations your way. You are more awesome than you think.

YOU ARE WORTHY.

Chapter Reflection:

You are God's chosen seed laid down on fertile soil. How are you planning on watering your seeds with these daily doses of inspirations?

My three, I AM, affirmations for this week are?

I AM...

I AM...

I AM...

My three unique qualities are?

1.

2.

3.

CHAPTER 7:

THE CONCLUSION: CALLED BUT NOT AFRAID

Co-author, Connie Ajah-Ayang, says, "You may wonder what it means to be 'called' or 'chosen.' Who's really a part of the 'called' and 'chosen?' Why is nursing sometimes referred to as 'a calling,' and not just a profession?

You may often hear people ask, 'What is God calling me to do next?' In a religious context, Christians speak about being 'called.' When they say 'a calling,' they mean they feel as if God has chosen them for a specific job, function or assignment. They fulfill a task that is chosen by God, and assigned to only specific people. No one else can answer those calls from God, but them.

When you first enter the profession, you – like many of us – will be asked, "Why did you choose nursing?" Why *did* you choose nursing? There is often a variation of reasons, but the most prevalent reason is that, "Nursing is more than just a job, It's more than just a profession.

Nursing is my calling." My co-author, Gifty, and I agree with those statements. Nursing is more than just a career. It is a calling.

Many of us often take care of our families or friends when they get sick at home, right? Yes! But, it's an entirely different experience when you must take care of a total stranger. This stranger doesn't know you and you don't know them, but you are required to get into their personal spaces. You often meet them in their most vulnerable states. And those people allow you to enter that space and care for them, and you do so as if you were their family. It's a totally different experience, and not everyone can do it. Not everyone is called to be a nurse and carry out those duties. Nursing requires a special grace, and a compassionate and empathetic heart. Now, you can understand why Nursing is a calling.

The pandemic has been and is presenting nurses with new challenges to our Calling. We had to answer the call, even when it meant braving dangerous and uncertain places. But, we're not afraid. We can't be afraid to do what we've been called to do – not now and not ever. We have been called more than ever during this pandemic, and we answered the call with resiliency, courage and fearlessness. Nurses all over the globe have stepped up and answered the call.

In the Bible, everyone that was called by God answered the call – regardless of if they were properly equipped for the assignment. David, who was a young shepherd boy called to be King, wasn't afraid of his new position or responsibilities. He answered God's call because He knew that God would support him. We are also supported by God.

No matter the circumstances, we can't be afraid to answer God's calling. "Why would we be afraid?" Well, taking on a new challenge can be hard, but scripture reminds us to not be afraid or fearful because God will always see us through to tomorrow. These phrases are written in the Bible many, many times. It is not a coincidence. It's God reminding us that he will hold on to us numerous times, and that we don't have to be afraid, anxious, or feeling dreadful because He is with us. He is always with us.

Throughout this pandemic, you've embraced providing excellent care to COVID-19 patients without hesitation. You've empathized with patients who felt like they were being isolated from the rest of the world and confined to only their hospital rooms. You've appreciated their loved ones who trusted you to provide the best care for them. Of course, the road hasn't been easy. The pandemic has pushed us all to the brink. Some days were obviously harder than others. Some days most of us were pushed to our breaking point. Some days you felt lost and cried. There were days when it seemed like your best just wasn't enough. But guess what? You're not broken. The pandemic didn't break you. You are here, today, reading this book because you haven't left Nursing in your heart. Remember that, you've held on. You are strong. You will survive. And you can overcome.

We want you to remember that you are called. You are chosen. And as you continue serving your patients, communities and nation, remember that answering the call to care is following God's Will. It's easy to follow God when you get what you prayed for or expected from him, but it's an entirely different story when you're called to follow Him without expecting what you want. This pandemic is one of those things we didn't expect to experience in our Calling, but we ought to remember that every crown comes with a cross to bear. As the pandemic rages on, many of us may lose hope in God but we have to remember that there are no testimonies in life without tests. This trial is an opportunity for us to grow in strength, courage and perseverance.

Bloom wherever you are planted for you are a seed of greatness. Know that your seed of greatness is still developing. The promise of restoration comes from the Lord. Trust that God's plans for you will always stand.

If there's anything we can all learn from this pandemic, it's to Live each day in the Moment, Find and Know your Purpose, Cultivate and Nurture important Relationships, and Enjoy every Second of your Journey. Life is a journey and not a destination. It's never too late to start. And as we continue in our journey, we must remember to stand firm on our Faith, hold onto the Truth of God's Words, and build on the principle of the triple FFF's.

And lastly, our hope is that this book will help you progress in your Faith. We hope that you develop a Firm Foundation in Faith, so that, when you are faced with challenges you can draw from this well to overcome anything. And whatever you do, Don't Stop Praying.

Chapter Reflection:

What have you learned from reading this book that can help you stand on a Firm Foundation in Faith?

REFERENCES

"Definition of faith in English". Oxford Living Dictionaries. Oxford University Press. Retrieved March 1, 2019.

"Positive Self-Talk." Support for Nurses & Midwives. Nurse & Midwife Support. Accessed November 26, 2021.

https://www.nmsupport.org.au/students-and-graduates/positive-self-talk#:~:text=Copright%20%C2%A9%202017%20Nurse%20%26%20Midwife%20Support.

"Someday You're Going to Look Back on All the Progress You've Made and Be Glad You Didn't Quit.: Fitness Motivation Quotes, Inspirational Quotes, Words." Pinterest. Accessed November 26, 2021.

https://www.pinterest.com/pin/741827369840784988/.

Winkelstein, Warren. "Florence Nightingale." *Epidemiology* 20, no. 2 (2009): 311. https://doi.org/10.1097/ede.0b013e3181935ad6.

ABOUT THE AUTHORS

Connie Ajah-Ayang

Connie Dione Ajah-Ayang is a Mastered Prepared Nurse with a Specialty in Nursing Informatics. She has been in the nursing field for thirteen years and is currently a Nurse Informatics Specialist/Analyst. Connie obtained a Bachelor's Degree in Law and Political Science, from the University of Dschang, in Cameroon, West Africa, in 2001. She received a Bachelors (BSN) from Delaware State University in 2008 and a Master of Science (MSN) in Nursing in 2015 from Walden University. She also holds a Bachelors's (LLB) in Law and Political Science and a certification in Medical-Surgical Nursing.

Connie loves spending time with family, reading, traveling, watching movies, shopping, writing, fitness, wellness, fellowshipping, and politics. In addition, she has a passion for inspiring and motivating people, either by words, videos on social media, or written content.

She is the spiritual leader of the Victory Women of Dover prayer group and plans and coordinates spiritual retreats for the group and mentorship on faith and spirituality. In addition, she is a member of the community outreach committee for the newly created Caregiver Support Foundation, Inc., a 501(c)3 organization. Their mission is to provide support and resources to caregivers to achieve their highest level of physical, emotional, and mental wellbeing while taking care of their loved ones.

Connie is married to Bruno Ayang and has two amazing boys, Jayden Ayang and Avery-Jayce Ayang. They reside in Dover, Delaware.

Gifty D. Boateng

Gifty D. Boateng was born in Kumasi-Ghana, West Africa, the only girl among four wonderful brothers. She was named Gifty, which means "Gift from God"; Gifty is a servant of God, wife, mother, philanthropist, coach, and a mentor to many.

Mrs. Boateng has been a nurse for 18years and holds a Master's Degree in Nursing. She graduated from Delaware State University and is a member of the Delaware Organization for Nurse Leaders (DONL), Society of Nurse Scientists, Innovators, Entrepreneurs, and Leaders (SONSIEL).

She's very passionate about the ministerial work that God has called her to do with caring for others, especially those in need. She serves her patients and community with integrity, compassion, kindness, and strives for excellence. She's the founder and CEO of Global Ubuntu Impact Foundation(501c3) and Co-founder of Noble Nurses Network.

She has been involved in several community outreach programs, health fairs and donated items to the less privileged population in the USA and Ghana. Many who know Gifty can describe her as God's gift because she keeps giving unto others to make an impact for the glory of God.

Mrs. Boateng loves spending quality time with her family and loved ones; she enjoys fellowshipping, serving at the Father's House, dancing, singing, shopping, networking, walking, volunteering, and having fun.

Mrs. Boateng is married to her God-fearing, wonderful husband, Mr. Boateng, and has two miracle babies, Samuel Adom (Grace) and Emmanuelle Nyameye (God is Good). They currently reside in Dover, Delaware.

Made in the USA
Middletown, DE
04 March 2022